A Stepping-Stone Book

From Scrolls to Satellites
The Story of Communication

By William Wise

Pictures by Hans Zander

Parents' Magazine Press • New York

Contents

How We Communicate

Every day, you talk and listen to your family, your friends, or your teachers. When two or more people talk together, they are communicating with one another.

When you tell someone that you are hungry or thirsty, you are communicating information about yourself. When your teacher tells the class a story about people in Canada or Africa, she is communicating information about those who live in another part of the world.

There are many ways to communicate. Mostly we do it with words. We use words when we speak, write, and read. The writer of this book is trying to communicate with you now. He is using words to tell you certain things. But you must read and understand his words, before he *really* can communicate with you.

Sometimes, instead of speaking, we communicate by using other kinds of sounds. When a factory whistle blows, it tells the workers that it is time to go to work, or that it is time to go home. When a fire engine comes down the street, its siren is a signal that tells us of danger.

Sometimes we see a signal, instead of hearing it. The traffic light is a signal we see every day.

When the light is red, it tells us not to cross the street. When the light turns green, we know it is safe to cross.

In today's world, we can communicate quickly with people nearby, or with people far away. When we need help, we can telephone the doctor, the fire department, or the police. When someone in our family goes away for a visit, we can call him on the telephone. We can talk with him in the next town, or halfway across the country.

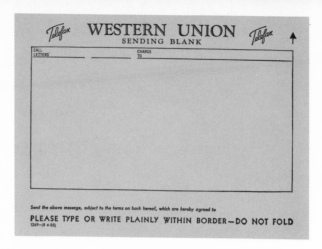

When we have a short message for someone far away, we may send it by telegram. When we have a longer message, we may send it by regular mail, or by air mail.

In today's world, we can use communications to have fun. We can enjoy music on the radio. We can watch baseball, basketball, and football games on television. We can read stories in magazines, or watch them being acted on television or in the movies.

We also can use communications to learn something. We can find out the latest news from newspapers, radio, or television. Sometimes

communication makes our lives safer. When a
heavy snowstorm or a hurricane is coming, the
radio or television warns us ahead of time, so
that we will be ready for it.

Our libraries have books that we can read.
Many of these books will help us to understand
people who are different from ourselves. Many
will tell us how people used to live, and what they
thought, in other times besides our own.

But when men first began to live in the world, it was not easy for them to communicate with one another. They could not read or speak as we do. If they learned something important, they had no way of writing it down so that their children and grandchildren could learn it, too.

Until people found out how to communicate more easily, no one could hope to understand much about the things around him. For thousands of years men lived this way, in a world that was very, very different from our world today.

The Way Language Grew

Many thousands of years ago, men learned to tell stories by painting pictures on the walls of their caves. Afterwards, people could look at the pictures, and "read" what the stories were about. In this way, ideas first began to be handed down, from the old to the young.

The earliest men probably could only "speak" to one another by making grunting noises and other simple sounds. Little by little, though, these sounds became words, and then sentences. Finally people in different parts of the world began to speak their own languages.

The use of the spoken word was an important step forward. More information could now be shared, and life was made a little easier.

It took people even longer to learn how to write. In a place called Mesopotamia, men wanted to keep records of the things they owned. So they began to "write," by drawing pictures of fish, birds, and other animals. Each picture had a different meaning. The men stamped these picture-signs into small tablets of wet clay. Then they baked the clay in the sun until it became hard. After that the clay tablets could be "read" by anyone who knew what the picture-signs meant.

As the years went by, more and more picture-signs were used. Finally the people of Mesopotamia had a picture-language that could be written and read.

In the nearby land of Egypt, people did not
write on clay. A water plant, called papyrus, grew
in Egypt. Men learned how to make papyrus into
a kind of paper. They also learned how to make
ink. After that they used papyrus-paper to write
down messages, stories, and numbers. When they
finished writing, they rolled up their pieces of
papyrus and stored them away.

These pieces of papyrus were called "scrolls."
They took up less room than the clay tablets.
And they were easier to carry around, because
they did not weigh as much.

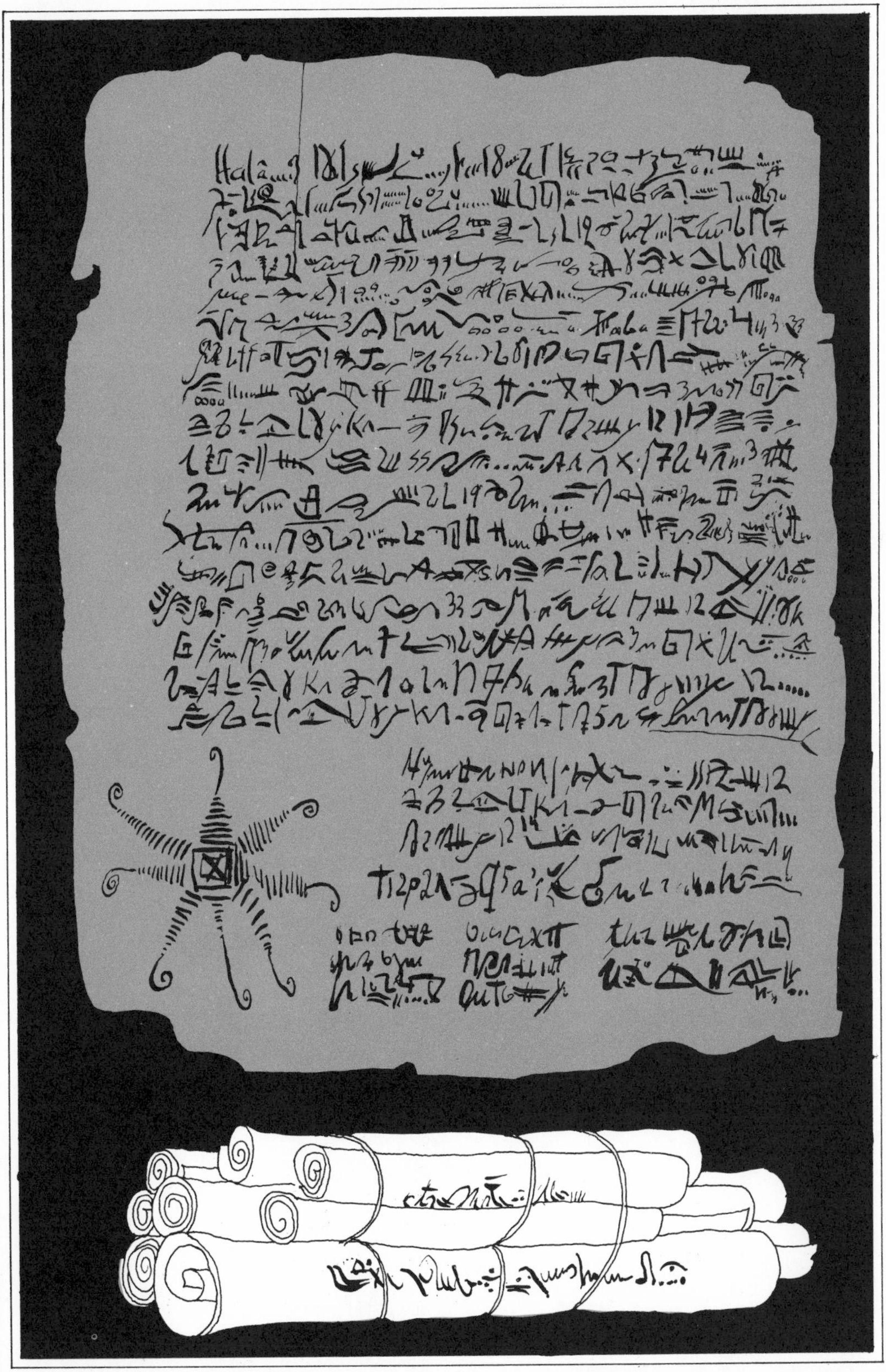

The Greeks were a sea-going people. Some of them sailed to Egypt, where they learned about papyrus-paper. Soon they were using papyrus scrolls to write on.

They wrote down the plays they acted in their outdoor theaters. They wrote down long poems about battles and heroes. They wrote about history and travel, about the stars and the sea. In a few years the world's first libraries were filled with what they had written.

The Romans lived after the Greeks. They also wrote a great deal, and had large libraries. But in time the Romans were defeated by their enemies. After that many Greek and Roman papyrus-scrolls were destroyed.

For the next thousand years, hardly anyone in Europe could read or write. There were not many books, either. A few monks made copies of some Greek and Roman writing. They wrote on a stiff material called parchment. But they worked so slowly that books were still very rare until about five hundred years ago.

Then, in Germany, Johann Gutenberg invented the printing press. Other men also learned how to print books. Before long, printers were at work in many cities. Paper-making already had been invented in China. Now, all over Europe, paper, instead of parchment, began to be used in printing.

As the years passed, more and more people learned how to read and write, and more and more books were printed. In time, small newspapers began to be printed, too. People no longer had to live without knowledge and information. They could read stories, poems, and books of science. They could read the news in their papers, and learn what men were saying and doing in other parts of the world.

In our own day, new inventions have made printing many times faster and cheaper. Millions of newspapers, magazines, and books are printed each year. Now we can learn about almost anything that interests us, and we can easily share what we learn. People can understand one another, and can begin to work together to build a better world.

Johann Gutenberg's invention made all these things possible. But it did not solve one old and important problem. How could messages and other information be sent without delay across great distances?

Signals and Messages

Even in the earliest times, people had tried
different ways of communicating quickly.
Sometimes they sent letters by messenger.
Sometimes they communicated by using signals.

Greek soldiers sent messages by turning their
shields toward the sun. The flashes of reflected
light could be seen several miles away. The enemy
did not know what the flashes meant. But other
Greek soldiers understood what the message said.

In some places, Roman soldiers built long rows of signal towers. When they had a message, the soldiers shouted it from tower to tower. If there were enough towers, and enough soldiers with loud voices, important news could be sent over a long distance.

American Indians used smoke signals to send messages. First they built a smoky fire on the top of a hill. Then they held a blanket over the fire. Each time the blanket was lifted, a puff of smoke rose in the air. Watching on a second hill, other Indians counted the number of puffs and understood the message.

In Africa, men learned to send messages by
beating on a series of large drums. Each drum was
kept within hearing distance of the next one.
The drum beats were sent out in a special code
that all the drummers understood. Though the
messages were simple, they could be sent at
great speed for hundreds of miles.

In Europe, men found another way to send
short messages. They built towers, and signaled

one another by using a semaphore. Each position of the arms had a different meaning, known to the men who worked the semaphore.

For thousands of years, men sent messages by all of these different means. But as little as two hundred years ago, most people in the world still could not communicate quickly enough.

To call a doctor or to ask help in fighting a fire, you had to go on foot. Mail service was very slow. Letters went by mail-coach, or were carried in the pockets of a single horseback rider.

On land, letters or messages hardly ever traveled faster than the speed of a horse. At sea,

nothing traveled faster than the speed of a sailing ship. Everywhere there was a need for faster communications.

At times, people suffered a great deal because information could not be sent quickly. In the year 1815, a terrible battle was fought near the city of New Orleans between American and British soldiers. Only later was it learned that the battle should never have been fought. Both sides had agreed to make peace—two weeks *before* the first shot had been fired. But word of peace had traveled too slowly. More than a thousand soldiers had been killed or wounded by the time the news arrived.

Morse's key

"A Patient Waiter Is No Loser"

In 1832, an American painter named Samuel Morse left England to return home. Morse had long been interested in fast communications. One evening aboard his ship, he heard another passenger talking about electricity. The passenger told him how an electric current could be made, and how far and how quickly the current would flow along a wire.

That night Morse hardly slept. He seemed to see wires stretching around the world carrying messages at great speed. For Morse realized almost at once that the flow of an electric current could be controlled, simply by raising and lowering a key at one end of a wire. And then, by stopping and starting the current, messages could be sent.

Aboard the ship, he worked out a code of short and long signals, called "dots" and "dashes." Later, Morse improved his code. Today, it is known as the International Morse Code. Here it is:

The International Morse Code

Alphabet

A.	.-	H.	....	O.	---	V.	...-
B.	-...	I.	..	P.	.--.	W.	.--
C.	-.-.	J.	.---	Q.	--.-	X.	-..-
D.	-..	K.	-.-	R.	.-.	Y.	-.--
E.	.	L.	.-..	S.	...	Z.	--..
F.	..-.	M.	--	T.	-		
G.	--.	N.	-.	U.	..-		

Numbers

1.	.----	6.	-....
2.	..---	7.	--...
3.	...--	8.	---..
4.	....-	9.	----.
5.	.....	10.	-----

Back in America, Morse built the first model of what he called the "telegraph." He found it hard, though, to interest anyone in his invention. He was poor, and always needed money. To keep from starving, he taught art at college.

One of Morse's students became interested in the telegraph. The student's father was rich, and gave Morse enough money to build a small laboratory. There Morse and the young student built a better model. When it was ready, the student's father came to the laboratory. He didn't believe the invention would work. He wrote a message on a slip of paper: "A patient waiter is no loser."

"Send that to Professor Morse," he said, "and see if he gets it at the other end!"

His son began to tap out the message with his telegraph key. In the next room, Morse received the signals, and wrote down the message. Then he carried it back and showed it to the student's father. He had written, "A patient waiter is no loser."

Luckily, Morse himself was a patient man. From 1838 to 1844, he tried to get the first telegraph line built. He showed people his model and proved that it worked. But businessmen did not think the telegraph would be very useful. Neither did President Martin van Buren and his Cabinet, when Morse showed them how easy it was to send messages "instantly" over a wire.

Morse went to England, France, and Russia. None of these countries was willing to spend the money to build a telegraph line. At last, back home, Congress agreed to give him $30,000 to build a test line from Washington to Baltimore.

At this point, with success so near, Morse made a mistake. He laid his wire underground in pipes. The wires were not insulated, though, which meant that the electric current could escape freely into the ground. The wire "went dead"— it would not carry a message. More than $20,000 had been spent, and there was nothing to show for it.

Samuel
F. B. Morse

But Morse still had almost $10,000. This time, he and his helpers strung the wire above ground on poles. To keep the electricity from escaping, they insulated the wires with the necks of glass bottles. At last the test line, just forty miles long, was ready.

A friend of Morse dictated the first message in Washington. "What hath God wrought?" the message said.

The letters were tapped out, and at the other

end of the line, the Baltimore operator received them. Newspaper reporters crowded around, as the telegraph key clicked away. Finally the operator handed them the message: "What hath God wrought?"

In a few seconds, a message in dots and dashes had been sent from one city to another. Before long, telegraph lines were strung between other cities, both in America and Europe. The age of rapid communications had begun.

Since then, other inventions have been developed, like the telephone, the radio, and the teleprinter. These inventions now do much of the work first done by Samuel Morse's telegraph. But for many years the wires he had dreamed of *did* stretch around the world, carrying messages at great speed.

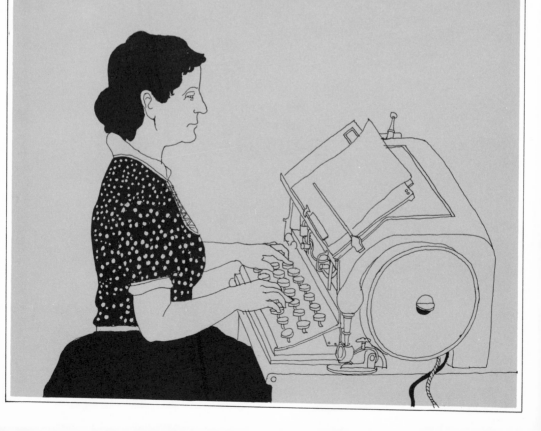

The Pony Express

It took time and money to build new telegraph
lines, and for a number of years there were many
parts of the United States that still had no
telegraph service. When gold was discovered in
California, thousands of men hurried there from
the East. After they arrived, they wanted letters
and news from home. Expert riders soon began
to carry newspapers and mail between the
Mississippi River and the gold fields of California.

Many of the riders were teen-age boys. Mounted on the fastest horses in America, they became known as the Pony Express.

Never before had there been a mail service like the Pony Express. The route, across prairie, mountain, and desert, was almost 2,000 miles long. From St. Joseph, Missouri, it ran west to Sacramento, California. The "home" stations on the trail were seventy-five to a hundred miles

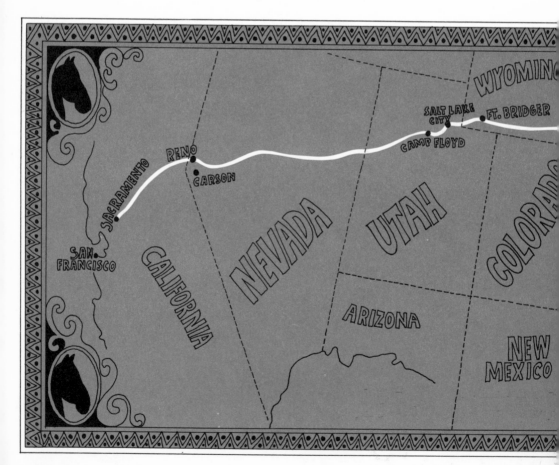

apart. Each rider sped back and forth between his two home stations. On the way, he changed to fresh horses, which were kept at smaller stations along the trail.

Nothing seemed to stop the young riders of the Pony Express. Their goal was to carry the mail in ten days, from one end of the line to the other. Very often, in spite of terrible conditions, the mail arrived ahead of time.

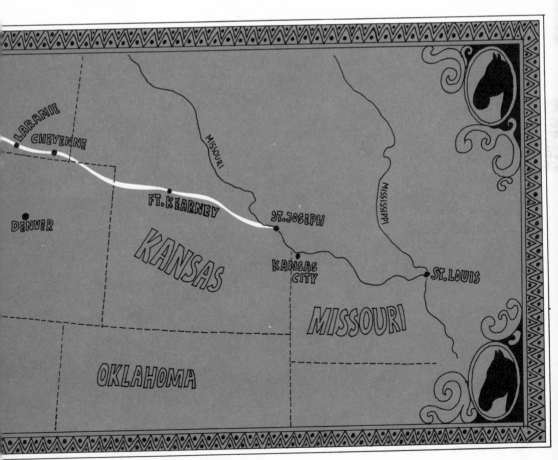

During the winter months, huge snow drifts filled the mountain passes. But the riders spurred their horses on through the worst blizzards. Usually they managed to reach their home stations, although more than one rider lost his way and froze to death.

In the summer, the Indians attacked both the stations and the riders on the trail. Several of the riders were killed, and many others had narrow escapes.

The Pony Express ran for only a year and a half. The owners of the line lost their money. But for eighteen months, before the telegraph came to the West, the people of California kept in touch with the rest of the country, through the most daring mail carriers the world had ever seen.

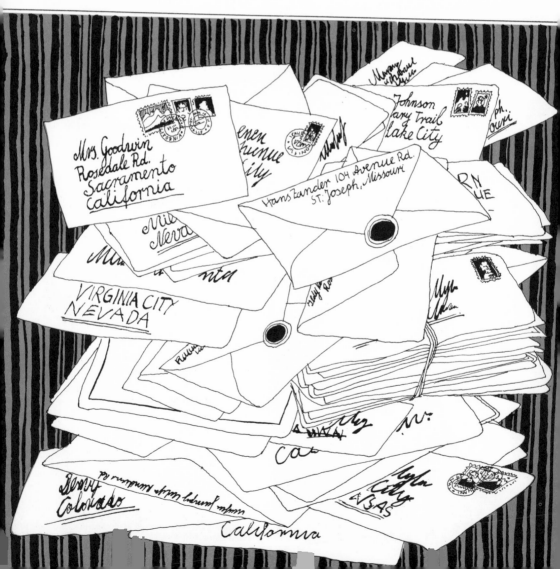

A Cable Under the Sea

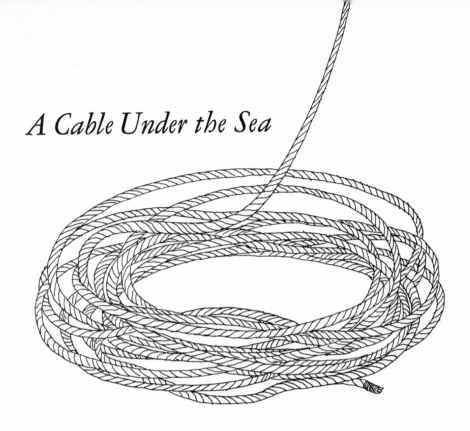

The great seas of the world always had kept men apart. Now, through the use of electricity, it seemed possible that messages might be sent across even the largest bodies of water.

For ten years, men worked to lay a 2,000-mile electric cable across the bottom of the Atlantic Ocean. Their leader was Cyrus W. Field, a young American businessman. Field saw the growing need for swift communciations. He knew other businessmen, and they helped him start a company to pay the cost of laying the cable.

The Atlantic Cable had to be very strong. On the bottom of the ocean there were rocks sharp enough to cut through regular wires. There were fish that could gnaw through almost any material. The cable that was strung had several strands of wire, twisted together. The strands

were wrapped inside an insulating cover of gutta-percha, a material very much like rubber.

The British and American governments worked with Field's company. In 1857, an American ship, the *Niagara*, sailed east, while the *Agamemnon*, a British warship, sailed west. Each ship carried half the length of cable. They were to meet in mid-ocean, and there splice the two parts together.

The *Niagara* was only five miles at sea when its cable broke. The ship returned to port, to start again. On the other side of the ocean, all went well for several days. Slowly, mile after mile, the cable on the *Agamemnon* unwound. But suddenly the ocean floor fell away a couple of thousand feet. Out the cable went, faster and faster, and finally it snapped.

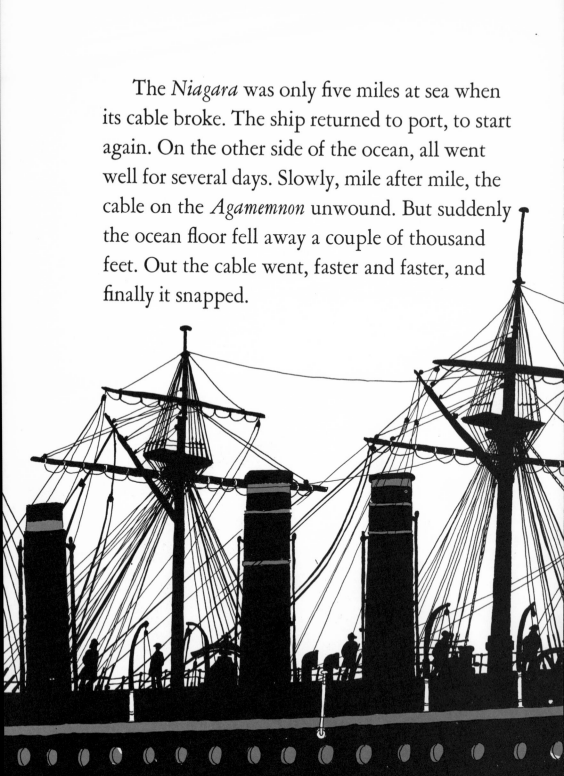

The next year, the two ships tried again.
A great storm came up and the *Agamemnon* almost
sank. She rode out the storm, but then, without
warning, her cable broke. Defeated, the two
ships sailed back to port.

Later the same year, Field sent his two ships
out to try once more. This time, they were able
to lay the cable from Newfoundland to Ireland.

45

Overnight, Field became a hero. There were parades and dinners in his honor. Messages of good will were exchanged by Queen Victoria of England and President James Buchanan of the United States. Their messages were sent in dots and dashes along the Atlantic Cable.

46

But the strands of wire were not strong
enough. The current began to fade. Soon the cable
went dead. Field and his men had failed again.

Then came the American Civil War. Field
could not make his next attempt until 1865, when
the war was over. That year he decided to use

the *Great Eastern*, the biggest ship in the world, to lay his cable.

The *Great Eastern* sailed from Ireland. The cable broke after 1,200 miles of expensive metal had been spooled out. Another year was over, and there had been another failure.

Field spent the fall and winter raising money. In July, 1866, the *Great Eastern* left Ireland a second time. The ship sailed to Newfoundland, unreeling a bigger cable than any used before. No accident took place, and when the line was tested, it worked perfectly. As the weeks and months passed, it went on working.

Cyrus Field finally had managed to lay a cable across the bottom of the stormy Atlantic Ocean. For the first time, Europe and America were linked together. Since then, other cables have been laid across almost every other ocean floor in the world, putting millions of people around the globe into "instant" communication.

"The Most Wonderful Thing in America!"

"The time will come when the human voice will be carried freely along a wire." Alexander Graham Bell was still a young man when he spoke those words. But, like most inventors, he had to wait a long time to prove that he was right.

Bell was born in Scotland, a sickly child with weak lungs. His family moved to Canada, where the air was better. In Canada, Bell studied sound

and the human voice, and became a teacher.
Then he was invited to come to Boston, to help
children who had trouble speaking.

In Boston, Bell became interested in electricity.
Why, he wondered, did messages have to be sent
in dots and dashes? Why couldn't the sound of
the human voice be sent along a telegraph wire,
so that two people could talk together?

Bell asked a number of experts, but they all
shook their heads. "Impossible," they told him.
"It can't be done."

Using wires, magnets, and electric batteries,
Bell began to build models of an invention

he called the "telephone." None of his ideas worked. Then one day Bell's assistant happened to pull a small spring connected to their latest model. In another room, listening into the receiver, Bell heard a faint "twang." It was the first sound ever heard over a telephone line.

Month after month, Bell and his assistant tried out new ideas. At last, in 1876, Bell took his invention to the Philadelphia Exposition. But many other inventors came there, too, and no one paid any attention to the telephone.

Late one hot summer afternoon, a group of men walked by Bell and his model. One of them was Dom Pedro, the Emperor of Brazil.

Out of politeness, the Emperor agreed to sit down and "try" the telephone. He put the receiver to his ear. At the other end of the table, Bell said a few words into the speaker.

"God save us—it talks!" the Emperor said.

Model of Bell's first Telephone

Several of the men in the Emperor's party understood a great deal about electricity. After listening to Bell's invention, one of them said, "It does talk! Gentlemen, this invention is the most wonderful thing in America!" The next day, the newspapers carried the story. After that,

Bell found it much easier to raise the money he needed.

Many years went by, though, before the telephone was widely used. In time, more and more phones were put into offices and homes, and distant cities and countries were connected by telephone lines.

In 1915, America's first coast-to-coast service was opened between Boston and San Francisco. In 1923, a call was made from London to New York. Four years later, regular service began across the Atlantic Ocean. Another service was opened between the United States, Australia, and South America, in 1930.

Now almost every country in the world can be reached quickly by telephone. Over the years, few inventions have meant more to people everywhere.

Today, perhaps no single means of communication is more important than "Hot

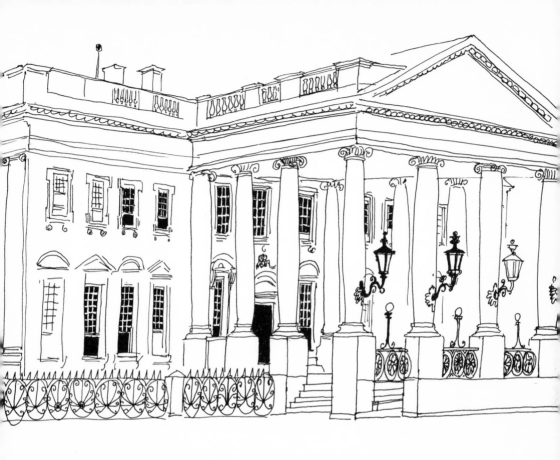

Line" telephones. One connects the White House
in Washington with the office of the Chancellor
of West Germany, in Bonn. Another connects
the White House with the Kremlin Palace in
Moscow. This Hot Line makes it possible for the
President of the United States and Russia's
leaders to speak quickly to one another, whenever

the need arises. Without loss of time, any new or dangerous problem can be talked about. By using the Hot Line, both countries should find it easier to understand each other. A single telephone line might play an important part in helping to keep the world at peace.

Communications Today and Tomorrow

Within the last fifty years, so many new means
of communication have been developed that
it would take several books like this one to tell
about them all.

In 1918, America's first air mail pilots began
to fly the mails. They flew in small planes made
of wood. Landing fields had no lights, and there
was little advance weather information. Many
pilots were killed, before flying conditions were

made safer. Today, letters can be sent swiftly and safely, in jet airliners, from any city in America to almost any place on earth.

The invention of radio brought news, music, and sports events into the homes of people everywhere. Silent movies, and then the "talkies," gave us a new kind of entertainment. Television changed the living room into a private theater. Now, with the use of radio-controlled satellites that fly high above the earth, pictures of important

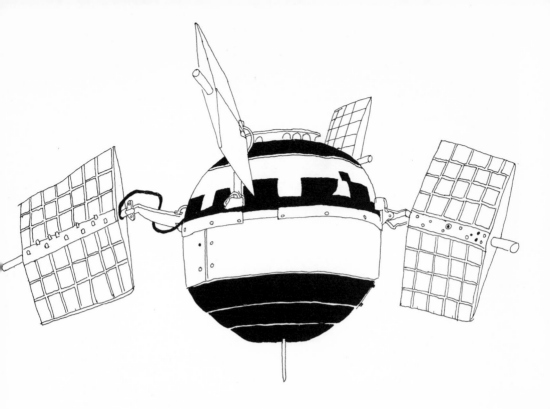

events can be flashed quickly across the seas.

In 1969, the first astronauts landed on the
Moon. Millions of people all over the world
watched and listened to their flight. Millions
heard the astronauts, while they were on
the Moon, talking over radio-telephone with the
American president back on Earth. Each year
our world grows smaller, and people in every
country are being drawn closer together, through
the wonders of modern communications.

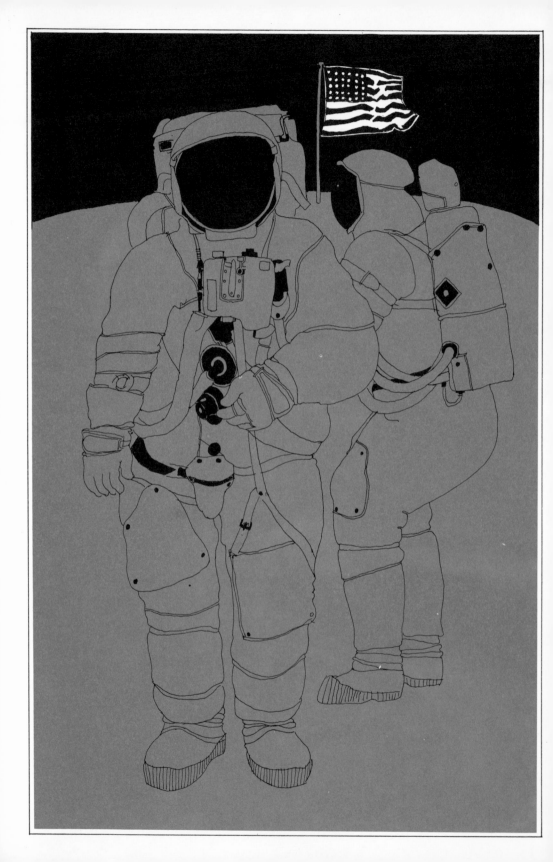

No one can say for certain what changes in communications the future will bring. We can guess, though, what certain things will be like. Satellites will continue to fly beyond the earth, taking pictures of the Moon, Mars, and the more distant planets. From these pictures, and from other information sent back, too, we will learn a great deal about the universe in which we live.

There will be computer-libraries, where tapes and other inventions will be stored. These

libraries will be filled with information. The words of a thousand books will be packed into a tiny bit of material.

There will be new inventions, connecting homes, offices, hospitals, factories, and libraries. By pushing a button, or turning a dial, a man will have all the information he needs within a few seconds.

In the world to come, communications will be faster than they are today. There will be new ways of sharing knowledge. Perhaps people will decide to use this knowledge wisely. If they do, the world will become a better place to live in than it has ever been, during all the years since men first painted pictures on the walls of their caves, and wrote on papyrus scrolls in the land of Egypt.

Index